The Astral Projection Series:
The Pineal Doorway

The Astral Projection Series

The
Pineal Doorway

Oliver Fox

Wright-Hyland Group

Astral Projection Series
The Pineal Doorway
Oliver Fox

Published 2019 by:
Night Swimming Press / Wright-Hyland Group

Printed in U.S.A.

ISBN: 9781689988490

"After death we live for some time in the astral world in the astral body used during our life on earth, and the more we learn to control and use it wisely now the better for us after death."

– Annie Besant

"Death is but an aspect of life, and the destruction of one material form is but a prelude to building up of another."

– Annie Besant

Also Available by Oliver Fox:

Astral Projection:
A Record of Out-of-the-Body Experiences

Table of Contents

PART ONE:
THE PINEAL DOORWAY

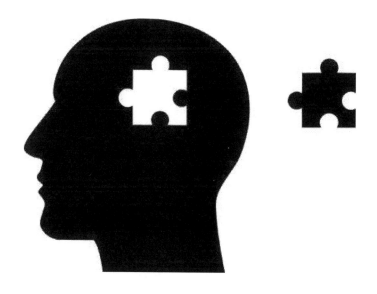

I. Introductory

I n writing this very condensed account of my practical researches into the little-known realms of dream-consciousness, astral travelling, and self-induced trance, I shall risk seeming egotistical and employ the first person. For one thing, it is far
more convenient; and for another, I wish to emphasize the purely
personal nature of this record — which is intended to be specula-
tive and not dogmatic. I do not profess to be an authority; but I
have, at least, for many years pursued a certain line of investigation, albeit in a somewhat desultory fashion, with long gaps of in-

activity. I write in the hope that my experiences may prove helpful to other students on the perilous way, and I need scarcely say that I shall be most glad to receive any additional information they can give me. I should like to supplement this bare account with many extracts from my notebook, but considerations of space render this impossible. I will now state the final result of my research and the two standpoints from which it may be viewed:

(a) *Scientific:* It is merely a new brain state, the product of self-induced trance, and the seeming external experiences all originate within the mind of the investigator — a third level of consciousness, differing from both waking life and ordinary dream, and far more vivid.

(b) *Occult:* The spirit actually leaves the entranced physical vehicle and functions — perfectly aware of so doing — apart from it upon the astral plane, the transition from normal waking life being achieved without any break in consciousness.

II. The First Step

*T*o acquire, by observing some incongruity or anachro-
nism, the knowledge that one is dreaming.

Eighteen years ago, when I was a student at a technical college, a
dream impelled me to start my research. I dreamed simply that I was
standing outside my home. Looking down, I discovered that the
paving-stones had mysteriously changed their position — the
long sides were now parallel to the curb instead of perpendicular

to it. Then the solution flashed upon me: though that glorious summer morning seemed as real as real could be, I was *dreaming!* Instantly the vividness of life increased a hundredfold. Never had sea and sky and trees shone with such glamorous beauty; even the commonplace houses seemed alive and mystically beautiful. Never had I felt so absolutely well, so clear-brained, so divinely powerful. Verily the world had become my oyster. The sensation was exquisite beyond words; but it lasted only a few moments, and I awoke. As I was to learn later, my mental control had been overwhelmed by my emotions; so the tiresome body asserted its claim and pulled me back. And now I had a (for me) wonderful new idea: Was it possible to regain at will the glory of the dream? Could I *prolong* my dreams.

I have italicized the heading to this section. It sounds simple; but in practice I found it one of the most difficult things imaginable. A hundred times would I pass the most glaring incongruities, and then at last some inconsistency would tell me that I was dreaming; and always this knowledge brought the change I have described. I found that I was then able to do little tricks at will, levitate, pass through seemingly solid walls, mould matter into new forms, etc.; but in these early experiments I could stay out of my body for only a very short time, and this dream-consciousness could be acquired only at intervals of several weeks. To begin with, my progress was very slow; but presently I made two more discoveries:

(1) The mental effort of prolonging the dream produced a pain in the region of the pineal gland — dull at first, but rapidly increasing in intensity — and I knew instinctively that this was a warning to me to resist no longer the call of my body.

(2) In the last moments of prolonging the dream, and while I was subject to the above pain, I experienced a sense of dual consciousness. I could feel myself standing in the dream and see the scenery; but at the same time I could feel myself lying in bed and see my bedroom. As the call of the body grew stronger the

dream-scenery became more faint; but by asserting my will to remain dreaming I could make the bedroom fade and the dream-scenery regain its apparent solidity.

And at this stage of my research a new query arose: what would happen if I disregarded the warning pain and fought it to a climax? As a matter of fact I was horribly afraid of making the experiment, but a sense of destiny urged me on. After funking one or two opportunities, I made the battle and won. Just when it seemed I must be beaten, something went click in my brain; the pain vanished, and also the sense of dual consciousness. I was locked out in the dream, which was apparently the glorified counterpart of the seashore about a mile from my home. It was all very beautiful and absolutely real — so real that the idea of "waking up" seemed quite absurd — but my triumph was marred by an uneasy feeling that I was now to face quite new conditions. Two things worried me: I had no idea how time was passing on the physical earth, and I was evidently invisible to the few people who crossed my path. This experience was subtly different from my previous excursions; for no longer, did there seem to be the slightest link between me and that once-tiresome physical body. Came the thought: Was I dead?

I did not like it and willed to return, but nothing happened. I tried again and again, and nothing happened. Then I got frightened — the utter loneliness became dreadful — but I knew that a panic might prove fatal. I waited a little, then tried once more. Again there came that strange cerebral click, and instantly I was back in my body. But, though I could hear the clock ticking and my grandfather moving about the next room, I was blind and could not move a muscle; I could not even raise an eyelid. That was my first experience of the seeming cataleptic rigor of the self-induced trance. Inch by inch I broke it, and it was an agonizing business. As it was impossible to move my body as a whole, I concentrated upon moving my little finger; then finger by finger I got my whole hand free; and then my arm. This done, I gripped

17

the bedrail above my head and pulled hard. Suddenly the trance broke, my eyes opened, and I was free. I jumped out of bed with great joy, and immediately collapsed upon the floor, being overwhelmed by nausea. I felt ill for two or three days afterwards.

For a time this fright had a sobering effect, and then the rashness of youth broke out once more. Again I fought the pineal pain and went through a very similar experience, though this time the seeming cataleptic trance was not so difficult to break; but then my nerve gave out. I was in love, and life seemed sweet. I decided that I would continue my experiments; but that I would never again disregard the warning pain. And I think it was well for me that I came to this decision.

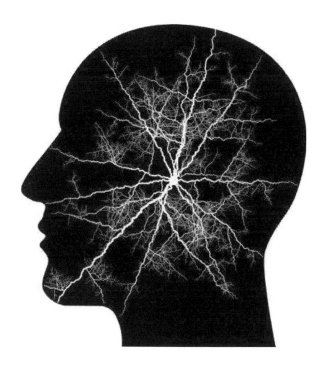

III. The Dangers

A s these are very real and great, I think I had better enu-
merate them before proceeding further with this record.
Any one who, without being under the guidance of an Adept or
Master, investigates on my lines exposes himself to the following
grave risks — at least, so I believe:

(1) Heart failure, or insanity, arising from shock. This dream-
world is very lovely, but it has its horrors also.

(2) Premature burial.

(3) Obsession.

(4) Severance of cord.

(5) Repercussion effects upon the physical vehicle, caused by injuries to the astral.

Of course the last three would be scorned by the orthodox experimenter. I would advise no one, motived by curiosity alone, to adopt my methods; for I know from experience that they are very dangerous. Yet would I not deter those students who feel themselves impelled by the driving force of Love, who seek to contact more closely the Great Soul of All — the Eternal Seven — Veiled Isis of the Universe. For though the astral plane is rightly termed the Realm of Illusion, yet is it one stage nearer to Reality, to the Ultimate Truth, than is this sad and solid illusion of the earth. Astral slums are horrible — terrifying, if you like — but not *sordid* as the slums of earth. There is glamour even in hell; for one senses there the divine Dark Face, which is one with the Shining; but here on earth both Faces alike are veiled so closely from the eyes of man. And that is why I pen this record for the few.

IV. The Second Step

T o distinguish them from the ordinary variety, I named
these dreams (in which I knew that I was dreaming)
Dreams of Knowledge. I come now to my next discovery, which
was that a Dream of Knowledge was often followed by a false
awakening, i.e. upon returning to my body I was under the im-
pression that I was awake, until some supernormal occurrence —
such as a sudden apparition — frightened me and caused me real-

ly to awake. I found then, after many experiences, that a Dream of Knowledge frequently led to a false awakening, in which my body was not dreaming in the ordinary sense, but was in a curious state, which I named the Trance Condition. These are its chief characteristics:

(1) The body appears to be in a semi-rigid condition, which may approach in severity the seeming cataleptic state already described.

(2) Though the eyes are closed, the room is plainly visible; and the atmosphere also, so that one gets an effect rather like particles of dust illuminated by the sun — or roughly, a golden glow, very variable in its intensity. Behind this, as it were, and only just on the borderline of visibility, is something like a mass of frog's eggs, bluish-grey in colour and vibrating.

(3) Physical sounds are distinctly audible.

(4) In this condition one is liable to any imaginable hallucination of sight or sound; or, to voice the other view, one is both clairvoyant and clairaudient.

(5), In this condition, especially if it be mistaken for the waking state, one falls an easy prey to wild and unreasonable fear.

(6) One is conscious of strange atmospheric stresses — the before-a-storm feeling, but enormously intensified.

On the whole this Trance Condition is extremely unpleasant and would probably deter many people if their chief motive were curiosity.

The question now arose: Can the Trance Condition be a prelude to a Dream of Knowledge as well as an after-effect? Time showed that the answer was, Yes. In those days I had not discovered how to induce the Trance Condition at will; but I occasionally found myself in it, sometimes before dropping off to sleep, sometimes after an ordinary or unremembered dream, and sometimes after a Dream of Knowledge. As I grew better able to recognize this state, so multiplied my opportunities for experimenting. I was getting things clearer and building very slowly my theory for liberating the soul at will ; but I did not yet realize that it was possible to pass from the Trance Condition into the Dream of Knowledge *without any break in consciousness*. When I found myself in the Trance Condition it served as a warning of what was to come; I knew the apparitions and strange objects, which I frequently saw, and the terrifying voices, to be astral and not physical, and would not let myself be sufficiently frightened to break the trance; it reminded me of getting past the "Dweller on the Threshold"; but always there was a break in consciousness before I found myself enjoying the glorious emancipation of the Dream of Knowledge. I never experimented without being afraid, and often panic spoilt my results. Through all those years it was a battle between fear and love of the unknown.

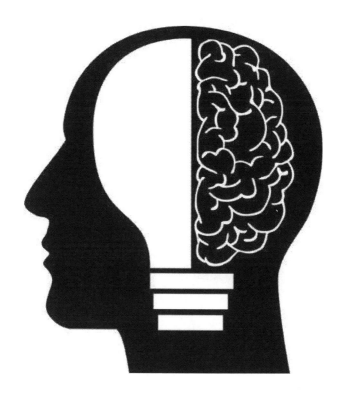

V. The Third Step

I t was meditating upon the warning pain, which I imagined to be located in the pineal gland, that led at last to my new discovery. In the ordinary way I could not step out of my body when in the Trance Condition. Before this was possible a mysterious something had to happen — and in those earlier experiments it probably occurred during the break in consciousness. And at last it flashed upon me what this something was: I had to force my incorporeal self through the doorway of the pineal gland, so that it clicked behind me. Then a further stage — a stage beyond the Trance Condition with its terrifying sensations; shapes and sounds — was reached. Then, and only then, could I step out of my physical body (now invisible), experience the dual consciousness, and be in the Dream of Knowledge (or a traveller on the astral plane) without any previous break in consciousness. It was done, when in the Trance Condition, simply by concentrating upon the pineal gland and willing to ascend through it. The sensation was as follows: my incorporeal self rushed to a point in the pineal gland and hurled itself against the imaginary trap-door, while the golden light increased in brilliance, so that it seemed the whole room burst into flame. If the impetus was insufficient to take me through, then the sensation became reversed; my incorporeal self subsided and became again coincident with my body, while the astral light died down to normal. Often two or three efforts were required before I could generate sufficient will-power to carry me through. It felt as though I were rushing to insanity and death; but once the little door had clicked behind me, I enjoyed a mental clarity far surpassing. that of the earth-life. And the fear was gone.

With a few exceptions, I never felt afraid once I had got clear of my body; it was the Trance Condition, before and after, that I dreaded. The tempest over, one passed into calm and sunlit waters. Leaving the body was then as easy as getting out of bed ; but I was always unable to see it — perhaps because its astral counterpart was withdrawn with me — though I could see my wife's form quite plainly. The dual consciousness was generally lost after I had left the house.

The reader is warned not to take my statements on the pineal gland too literally. The result I obtained is beyond all question; but my explanation of the actual process involved may be more symbolical than accurate. However, I have reason to suppose that I am not far out in my description, always remembering that things are only relatively true, and that the truth must ever elude the spoken or written word. And it is quite immaterial to the success of the experiment. By employing this method the result *can* be obtained.

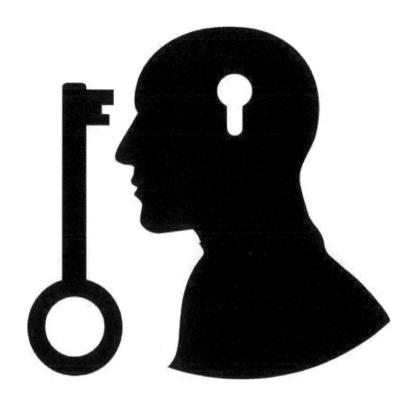

VI. The Fourth Step

N ow one thing was needed: to be able to pass at will into the preliminary Trance Condition. This was to prove most difficult to accomplish. The initial symptoms were fairly easy to produce; but the trouble was that this self-induced state was of such extremely short duration. The very slightest disturbance sufficed to break the trance in its early stages. Nine times out of ten this happened, and the trance was broken before it had become sufficiently deep to allow of any attempt being made to force the pineal door. And often when I had succeeded in inducing a strong trance I would suddenly lose consciousness and find myself, after an unremembered gap, free to move as I would upon the astral plane. Nevertheless, I have induced the trance and passed out through the pineal doorway 'without any break in consciousness whatever; and I have returned to my body to strengthen the trance and left it again and returned again, etc., as many as six times in one night, without a single break in the mental continuity of the experience. To induce the trance I would lie down, with muscles relaxed, turning my consciousness inward upon the pineal door and excluding all other thoughts; the body was passive, but the mind positive in its concentration upon this inner point. My eyelids were closed; but I believe the eyes were rolled upwards and slightly squinting — that was the sensation. The first symptom was the effect of seeing through my eyelids the room full of the golden light. Then came the numbness, beginning at the feet and extending upwards. When the trance was deep this became quite painful, especially in the muscles of the jaw; there was also a sense of enormous pressure in the brain.

This, then, was the climax of my research. I could now pass from ordinary waking life to this new state of consciousness (or from life to "death") and return, without any mental break. It is easily written, but it took fourteen years to accomplish.

VII. The Last Experiment

I n this paper I have in the main confined myself to a description of the methods adopted to obtain a certain result; but I shall not now deal any further with the result itself. If the Editor is agreeable and sufficient interest is shown, I might perhaps write a further paper, entitled "Beyond the Pineal Door." But as my experiments were terminated in a very curious and interesting way, I wish — if only for the sake of completeness to give a brief account of how I lost this power I had so painfully acquired.

In April, 1916, when out of the body, I attempted to get back into a past incarnation, which had been described to me by a lady who was an unprofessional trance medium. Now if I had willed to travel to India, I should have immediately rushed off with enormous velocity; but I willed to get back into my past life, and no motion occurred. Suddenly a gap appeared in the astral scenery (as though a round hole were made in a picture) and I saw very, very far away the open door of a temple, and beyond this a gleaming statue. This scene was blurred and had the appearance of being at the other end of a very long and narrow tunnel. I willed to pass through this tunnel, but found myself swept violently away, in a lateral direction, to some other astral locality. I willed once more; again the tunnel and the temple appeared; and again I tried to travel to it. This time, however, I was hurled back to my body, and with such force that the - trance was broken.

The next time I tried to induce the Trance Condition, I found that always before my inner eyes was the vision of a black *crux ansata*; and now my magic would not work; the trap-door *would not open*. The *crux ansata* could not be dispelled. When I closed my eyes and turned to the light, the symbol showed clear-cut, as though painted in black on the red field of my eyelids. With my eyes open, in a dim light, I could still see it as though it were projected in front of me. And try as I might I could no longer pass the pineal door.

Soon after this I started a long investigation into the powers of a most remarkable direct voice medium, who had, however, the rather unenviable reputation of being a black magician. In his company I had many astral adventures — after a break in consciousness I would find myself with him upon the astral plane — but I could no longer leave my body at will. And there I met and conversed with the group of spiritual beings who manifested through my friend. Their teachings were extraordinary; their spiritual grade seemed very high. I believe that they are real entities; but, despite their personal beauty and the charm of their language, I am not certain whether they are "white" or "black." They told me they had sealed my door, because I was becoming attuned to psychic forces, which might sweep me away before my work on earth was done. I do not know. *Some* things I have proved to myself; but each little advance we make serves only to emphasize the depths of our abysmal ignorance.

In 1915 the Army people had refused my services; but early in 1917 they changed their minds and kindly entrusted me with a pick and shovel — later, a rifle also. Through two and a half years of Active Service my black *crux ansata* kept me company, and I remained a prisoner in my body. Now I am back again, rather smashed up, and the scar upon my abdomen is roughly in the shape of a *crux ansata*. It seems the gods have a sense of humour. The visionary symbol still remains before my inner eyes, but it is now very faint and difficult to see. Perhaps when it has faded altogether my pineal door will open once again. I do not attempt to explain these happenings, but I have written a true account of them.

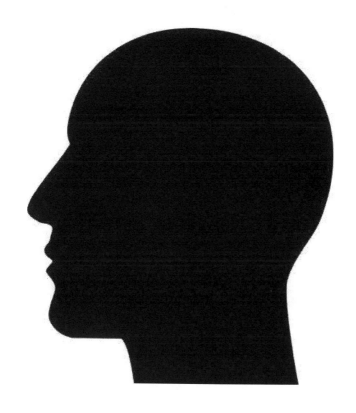

VIII. Concluding Note

P sychoanalysis is not exactly a new discovery, but lately it has penetrated into the penny populars. Mention dreams, and you are met with a triumphant "But Freud says—"! I think that some of my friends believed that if I read Freud I should die broken-hearted. Well, I have read Professor Siegmund Freud's great and admirable work — "The Interpretation of Dreams" — and it has not disturbed my equanimity. I think there is much truth in it, and I have applied his methods quite satisfactorily to interpret some of my ordinary dreams — especially the nonsensical kind. But there are dreams and *dreams*! I am convinced that the psychoanalytic theories will not explain all of them. I believe the Vienna doctor to be a kindly man with a mighty intellect, but even he does not know everything. For instance, I do not think he would admit that astrology "works"; but I know it does.

PART TWO:

BEYOND THE PINEAL DOORWAY

I. Introductory

This article is a sequel to "The Pineal Doorway" to which I must respectfully refer new readers, should my present remarks prove unintelligible. There I dealt with the method employed to obtain a certain result — which may be viewed either as an abnormal state of consciousness, or as a temporary release of the soul from its physical vehicle — and I am now going to give a few notes on the result itself. I fear this paper will appear, at best, only scrappy and inadequate but its very nature makes this unavoidable. The lonely explorer on the astral plane is up against so many difficulties that it is impossible for him to present a picture that shall be a clear and coherent whole. Struggling to withstand the pull of his physical body, often swept away against his will, like a leaf on the gale, by the mighty, unknown astral currents, he can only glimpse a little here and a little there; and even then, his memories fade with surprising rapidity — especially if the return to the body be in any way violent. The glamour lingers in his soul; but his records, the written words, the futile attempts to translate the untranslatable, seem so fragmentary and bereft of charm. In dealing with the result, I shall give, therefore, only a few rough notes on matters which appear to me to be of interest. Again I would emphasize this fact, that I employ the first person because it is obviously more convenient and because this is a purely personal record. I have been a practical investigator and a student of the occult; but I do not claim to be an authority on this or any other subject.

II. Locomotion

On the astral plane it is, of course, possible to walk, much the same as on the earth, though in favourable conditions the effort is almost negligible. When, however, the Trance Condition is becoming weak, and the pull of the body is consequently increasing in strength, while that mysterious pain in the region of the pineal gland gives its warning to return — then, walking is anything but effortless; it is as though one tugged against a rope of very strong elastic. Also one can employ any of the artificial modes of locomotion known to us on earth. People who cannot forget or forgive poor Raymond's cigar will get very cross with me when I say that there are electric trams on the astral plane; but there *are* — unless there is no astral plane, and my trains run only in my brain. But in this queer realm there are three additional ways of travelling, which gravity will not permit to ordinary mortals on the earth:

(a) Horizontal Gliding.

(b) Levitation.

(c) Skrying.

HORIZONTAL GLIDING

The gliding is accomplished by a purely mental effort, the arms and legs remaining passive. In my early experiments I found it difficult to get a start; but once started, the velocity was extreme, apparently ever increasing, until I arrived at my destination with a "silent bang." In other words, the last stage of the journey seemed too rapid to be comprehended, and suddenly *I was there* — as though I had fallen out of nowhere, or instantly materialized, on to this fresh scene. But on some occasions the line of my voluntary motion would seemingly encounter an opposing astral current, so that I would slow down and land quite gently — or even be carried back again if the current was too powerful for my will. I, with no guide to assist me, was always at the mercy of these astral currents or invisible streams of force. For example, I might will to travel to Xtown. I would start off, taking apparently the shortest occult cut, or line of least resistance, through houses, trees, etc. Flashing through these objects produces a dazzling and confusing effect, which acts like friction on one's mental energy and may be sufficient to break the trance. Well, if I was lucky, I would reach the astral counterpart of Xtown; but more often than not I would find myself swept away from my line of motion by a stronger astral current and borne to some strange destination. I might find myself in the beautiful grounds of a stately palace; but on the other hand, I might come to rest before a plump and pompous old gentleman in a white waistcoat, peacefully reclining in the bosom of his family, and quite unconscious of my unpardonable intrusion into his home life. At times these astral adventures became delightfully irresponsible — like one of Mr. Chesterton's romances anything might happen. But note this if that oracular old gentleman became so funny that I laughed outright, in the moment of giving way to my emotion I lost my mental control; my body whisked me back again, perhaps with such violence that the trance was broken and my experiment ended. When I returned to my body, either walking or gliding, of my own free will, I approached it in the normal way; but always, when it claimed me against my will, I experienced the sensation of being drawn *backwards* into it. In gliding, the feet seem to skim over the surface of the ground, or to be, at most, only a few feet above it.

LEVITATION

The other two modes of locomotion are both in the nature of levitation, although I believe them to be essentially very different: but that which I have called "levitation" is easy and harmless whereas the other method — which I have termed "skrying" — is difficult and dangerous, in my opinion. Bearing in mind this distinction, I will now describe the levitation. Please remember that I am dealing only with my own experiences, which have been consistently uniform, and that I do not wish to generalize or become dogmatic in my assertions. Unlike the skrying, my levitation was not accomplished by a purely mental effort; there was a downward pull, analogous to gravity, which had to be counteracted by a flapping motion of the hands; also I could not ascend

43

with my body perfectly vertical. Always I found that the same method was necessary: stand erect, arms to the sides, then let the body tilt backwards, so that it makes an angle of about sixty degrees with the ground; then move the hands with a gentle downward-beating motion. In this way one slowly rises to a height of, say, one hundred feet; the seeming gravitational pull is now much less, and it is possible to change from the backward-slanting position, so that one no longer travels feet first; forward motion can now be effected by movements of the arms similar to the breast-stroke in swimming, but the legs should be rigid. I found that, by this method, I could never rise to an apparent height of more than four hundred or five hundred feet; for beyond that I would suddenly experience a great increase in the downward pull. Also I could never "keep in the air" for more than a few minutes (?) at a time. I found this levitation very fatiguing; and the trance would sometimes be broken by what appeared to be a repercussion effect upon the physical body. The difference between this method of levitating and skrying will now become quite clear.

SKRYING

Skrying is like gliding, but in a vertical direction. There is no downward pull analogous to gravity, but only the call of the body. It is done by a purely mental effort, the arms being quite passive, and it is characterized by an enormous velocity of ascent. Levitation is a gentle floating, but in skrying one whizzes up like a rocket. I think it will be of interest if I now give an extract from my notebook, which deals with my first experience of skrying:

July 9, 1914, 9 a.m. — *Noon.* "Got into the proper Trance Condition again (having just returned from an astral excursion), *fully conscious* that I was in it. Left my physical body — phenomena as before — and passed out into the garden. I then decided that I would make my first attempt at skrying or rising through the planes. I stood erect, arms to my sides, and concentrating all my will-power in one supreme effort, I willed to ascend. The effect was truly surprising. Instantly the earth fell from my feet — that was how it seemed to me, because of the suddenness and speed of my ascent. I looked down on my home; it was now no bigger than a matchbox, and the streets were only thick lines separating the houses. I then noted that I was travelling in a slanting direction. I rectified this by an effort of the will, and continued to ascend straight up. Soon the earth was hidden by white clouds. Up and up and up — velocity ever increasing. The loneliness I felt was indescribable. Up and up and up. My consciousness was perfect except for one thing — I lost my sense of *time*. I might have been out of my physical body for a minute, or an hour, or even a day — I could not tell. Thoughts of premature burial assailed me. Up and up and up. The loneliness was dreadful; only those who have had a similar experience can realize what I felt. The blue of the sky had been gradually fading; but the brilliance of the light had not diminished — at least, to any marked degree. Now I saw a most awe-inspiring phenomenon: from a point on the zenith emerged a succession of shimmering, leaden-hued, concentric circles of light, ever spreading in huge ripples — as when a stone is thrown into a pond. At this sight I got really frightened, but I did not lose my self-control. Realizing that I had nearly reached the limit to my power of endurance, I willed to descend. Instantly the process was reversed; the sky grew blue again; earth came into sight through the veil of fleecy clouds, rose up to meet my feet; and so I passed once more into the house and gently entered my physical body. I then experienced a touch of catalepsy and had the illusion that my wife was embracing me, desperately trying to bring me back to life. Such illusions (from the physical standpoint) are often experienced by me in this Trance Condition before leaving my body or on returning to it. I broke the trance without much difficulty, and rose from the bed. It was noon; so the whole experiment (including the previous astral excursion) had lasted three hours. I felt no sickness or bad after-effects. Indeed I had an unusual sense of physical freshness and spiritual exaltation, which lasted for the rest of the day. Actually the sun was shining brilliantly throughout my experiment, and so it was in my experiences out of my body."

I have been told that, by using this method, it is possible to travel to other planets; but that it is extremely dangerous for a student who is not under the guidance of an adept. In skrying I have advanced no further than I did in this first experience; for my earthly responsibilities have forced me to exercise some prudence in pursuing these investigations. Before leaving this subject I should like to state that I read with interest the letter by Mr. Noble Iverson, published in the Occult Review. I hope my paper may prove helpful to him.

III. People

In ordinary dreams and in Dreams of Knowledge (in which I know that I am dreaming) I meet and converse with all sorts of people; but whenever I have passed in full consciousness through the pineal door, I have found:

(1) A total absence of elementals or other terrifying beings, such as the horrible creatures and freakish animals to be seen in the astral hells.

(2) That, though I may pass among crowds of people, I am almost invariably invisible to them. They cannot see me or hear my voice; but they can feel my touch if I deliberately experiment with that intention. Yet to do so is disastrous; for the start they give in their fright makes me start also, which has a repercussion effect upon the physical body and breaks the trance. However, if I do not concentrate my attention upon them, I can pass through their bodies without their becoming aware of my presence. Only very rarely have I been visible to another person and able to enter into conversation. And in these exceptional cases our talk has been of very brief duration; for the act of speaking conflicted with my mental control, and the trance was broken. The will to remain out of the body must never be relaxed throughout the whole experiment; if one forgets this even for a moment, by giving way to an emotion or taking too lively an interest in one's surroundings, the body immediately asserts its claim.

(3) In Dreams of Knowledge I have frequently encountered beings who were seemingly far above me in spiritual grade; but I have never met with such in my fully-conscious functioning on the astral plane after forcing the pineal door. In all these experiments I have seemed to be peculiarly isolated, meeting no superior intelligence, nor have I come across a fellow-investigator. It is as though I functioned all alone upon another plane of existence.

I do not attempt to explain these things; I simply record them. But I know that my experiences were real and that others can prove them by adopting the method given in my previous paper. It by no means follows that their experiences will be very similar to mine — for all I know, I may have been protected by invisible guides, despite my seeming isolation — but I believe they would approximate sufficiently closely to prove the truth of my record. I am not clairvoyant, clairaudient, or mediumistic in waking life; but it may be that my success in this research was due to some unknown psychic abnormality. I have no reason to suppose such is the case; but if it were so, my method might be impossible to one who did not possess the necessary development of whatever psychic organ is involved — perhaps of the pineal gland? I will now give another extract from my notebook:

Some time in the Autumn of 1913. "In the afternoon, intending to experiment, I lay down on the bed and succeeded in getting into the Trance Condition. I then proceeded to leave my body, dual consciousness being experienced until I had passed out of the house (by going through the closed doors); but on reaching the street I could not feel my physical body lying upon the bed. I had walked on for about a hundred yards, apparently unobserved by the few people about, when I was caught up in some strong current and borne away with great velocity. I came to rest on a beautiful but unknown common. There seemed to be a school-treat going on; for there were many children, dressed in white, playing games and having tea beneath the trees. There were also some adults present — in particular I noticed one old gipsy wom-an. Bluish smoke rose up from the fires they had lit, and a mag-nificent amber sunset cast a mellow golden glow upon the peace-ful scene. I walked on until I came to some red-brick houses, which evidently marked the limit of the common in that direc-tion. The front door of one of these houses was half-open, so I entered, curious to see if the inhabitants would become aware of my intrusion. At the end of the hall was a flight of richly-carpet-ed stairs. Up these I passed. Seeing a door ajar on the first land-ing, I entered and found myself in a comfortably-furnished bed-room. A young lady, dressed in claret-coloured velvet, was standing with her back to me, tidying her hair before a mirror. I could see that radiant amber sky through the window by the dressing-table, and the girl's rich auburn tresses were gleaming redly in this glamorous light. I noticed that the coverlet of the bed had a crumpled appearance and that there was water in a basin on the wash-stand.

"'Ah, my lady!' thought I, 'you too have been lying down, and now you are making yourself presentable for tea — or is it dinner?'

"I did not mind intruding upon her privacy; for she might have no existence outside of my brain, and I knew, from previous experiences, that there was small likelihood of my being visible to her. It occurred to me that I would stand just behind her and look over her shoulder into the mirror. I wanted to see whether it would reflect my face. I stood so close to her that I was conscious of a pleasant fragrance emanating from her hair, or perhaps from the soap she had recently used. In the mirror I could see her face — a good-looking one, I think her eyes were grey — but not the faintest indication of mine was visible.

"'Well,' I thought, 'you evidently cannot see me. Can you feel me?'

"And I laid a hand upon her shoulder. I distinctly felt the softness of her velvet dress, and then she gave a violent start — so violent that I in my turn was startled too. Instantly my body drew me back and I was awake, my condition being immediately normal — no duration of trance, or cataleptic sensations. No bad after-effects. The western sky was blue when I lay down; but on breaking the trance I saw that it was actually the same glorious amber colour it had been in my out-of-the-body experience."

Unfortunately I omitted the date of this experiment, though I wrote the account immediately afterwards; but if this lady really exists on the physical plane and should chance to read this article — which I fear me is highly improbable — in return for her evidence I will tender most profuse and humble apologies.

I said just now that I had not encountered any elementals beyond the pineal door; but I have seen some pretty fearsome specimens when in the Trance Condition. Here is an example met with on February 6th, 1916.

"Great forces seemed to be straining the atmosphere, and bluish-green flashes of light came from all parts of the room. I then caught sight of a hideous monster — a vague, white, filmy, formless thing, spreading out in queer patches, with bulbous pro-tuberances and snake-like tentacles. It had two enormous round eyes, like globes filled with pale-blue fire, each about six or seven inches in diameter."

But such things are, of course, quite harmless, provided one can conquer the intense fear they inspire. Nevertheless, the danger to a weak heart is obvious; for the shock is great.

In the previous article I mentioned that, when I was out of my physical body, I was never able to see it lying on the bed, though my wife's form has been plainly visible. Sometimes I have found that my wife's body also was invisible, and on these occasions I have met her a short distance away — apparently functioning in her astral vehicle. We have talked together; but on waking, she has had no recollection of the night's happenings. Unfortunately it is rare for her to have any vivid memories of her dreams. When I have thus met her out of the body, she has been easily recognizable, but subtly altered in appearance, and I have noticed a faint aura. In a few other cases I have seen what appeared to be an aura; but generally this is not noticeable with the people I meet beyond the pineal door.

IV. Scenery

In dreams, either with or without the knowledge of dreaming, I have explored various regions of the astral plane; so that I find I can assent, from my own experience, to many details given in occult works and good automatic writings, such as the wonderful Vale Owen Script. I could add my own notes to the literature on this subject; but in the present article I wish to confine myself to things as I have found them beyond the pineal door. What then are the general characteristics of the scenery which confronts the investigator who has passed *in full consciousness* through that mysterious inner trap? The answer is that, allowing for the divinely glamorous atmosphere, magical in its transforming quality — which can make even a prosaic steam-engine seem beautiful — this world beyond the pineal door is remarkably similar to the earth. One has, it is true, the extended powers of locomotion and that of penetrating seemingly solid objects, the marvellous mental clarity, the divine sense of well-being and power — one has all these; but the surroundings are really surprisingly like this world of ours, which the extracts I have given from my notebook tend to show.

Yet is there this difference; the astral counter-part (if such it be) of a city appears much larger than the earthly one; for in addition to its present structures and features are to be found buildings, monuments, etc., which have no present existence on the earth. Some of these may have existed in the past; and others I suspect to be very powerful thought-forms — or perhaps the astral foreshadowings of earthly buildings yet to come. To the uninitiated this will sound very nonsensical; but consider it this way — every enterprise has its horoscope, the key to the occult forces behind its inception. If you can become connected up with the psychic trail of the forces governing the Xtown Technical College, you may get a vision of the new buildings to be occupied by that institution in 1930 — which is what a psychometrist actually does. Was it not written long ago that Past, Present, and Future are in truth but *one*? Well, the astral plane is an infinite network of psychic trails, and Xtown, as a whole, also has its horoscope.

I do not wish to labour the point. To the astral explorer, then, Xtown will seem at once both familiar and strange, a curious blend of known and unknown, of old-style and new or ultra-new; and the general effect will be that the astral Xtown is much larger than the earthly one. And as far as my experiences go, the investigator, who makes his nth trip to the astral Xtown, will still find the same features (non-existent on earth) that puzzled him on his first adventure. But there is a point I wish to emphasize: though the scenery so closely resembles that of earth, buildings are more than buildings beyond the pineal door; they are living things. Let me quote again:

Dec. 14th, 1913. "No one was abroad but me, though it was bright daylight, the cloudless sky being a delightful pale azure. So I emerged into a mighty square, and there before me towered a colossal building — a miracle of bulk and architectural beauty. Roughly it was Gothic in design, a mass of lacework and carven detail, with innumerable pointed windows and countless niches holding statues. The whole glowed with an indescribable mellowness, compounded of a thousand subtle shades and tints, in the wonderful brilliance and purity of the dream-light. This building was not only a thing of brick and stone; it seemed to be a living thing, to have an eternal soul; and for me it had all the high, intensely spiritual appeal of a lovely woman. That building alone might have inspired a novel, which one could call 'The Pinnacled Glory' — borrowing from Browning's *Abt Vogler*."

Utilitarians and Philistines scoff when a poet falls in love with some fair building; it seems such a "bloodless" thing to do! But the beautiful structure is the concrete expression on the material plane of a beautiful idea, and behind the idea there may be a still more beautiful being who gave it birth. The source might be "black?" Yes, but behind all things, behind the Dark Face and the White, and in all things, exists the One Supreme Life, the One Eternal Truth.

In these out-of-the-body excursions it would appear that one's powers of perception are enormously increased; and if inanimate objects seem endowed with life, how tremendously alive is the investigator himself, freed from his prison-house of matter But this strange quality of being alive does not make all the astral houses pleasing to the eye and soul. Far from it. Nevertheless, I have never found beyond the pineal door the horrible conditions and awful shapes, both human and non-human, which character-ize the astral hells; nor have I found there the vast museums, in-comprehensible machinery, and wondrous fantastically beautiful cities, which exist on other astral levels. As I have said, I am quite familiar with these "hells" and "heavens"; but never have I explored them, being fully conscious at the time of my precise condition and powers, after forcing my incorporeal self through the pineal door. I may have known at the time that I was dream-ing; but there is a vast difference between knowing it (in a theo-retical way) and *realizing* it, between finding oneself on the astral plane, after a break in consciousness, and passing there direct from waking life, with *no* break in the mental continuity.

It would seem, then, that this world beyond the pineal door oc-cupies a mid-position between the horrors of the astral hells and the fantastic beauties of the astral heavens; *extremes* have no place there; and, with the differences we have noted, it very closely resembles our earth. Now why is this? Is it really so, be-cause of some unknown conditions which limit the field of ex-ploration? Or is it only that my opportunities for investigation have been so few? I cannot attempt to answer this question. For me, it remains one of the most puzzling problems of the whole research.

In the astral world, we are told, the light varies according to the level of the subplane and the spiritual grade of the beings functioning thereon; but what of this realm that forms the subject of my paper? Is it day there when it is day on earth? As far as my researches go, the answer is, Yes. I have often noticed, on com-ing out of the Trance Condition, that the "real" sky was the same as the "dream" sky I had just left, though the original sky, ob-served before entering the Trance Condition, might have been quite different. This has been my experience with regard to places familiar to me; but sometimes when the place has been quite strange, I have found it was day there, though night here in England. And, of course, if the unknown place chanced to be somewhere in the region of the antipodes, or five or six hours ahead of us, this would be the case. One night I apparently reached some strange Indian city, crowded with natives, though a few Europeans were present — and there it was bright day. Here I saw a curious fountain: a kneeling elephant, sculptured in black stone, ejected from its curled-back trunk a shower of water, which was caught in a white shell-shaped basin. To my knowledge I have never heard of, nor seen a picture of such a fountain. Can any one tell me if it exists upon the earth?

V. Conclusion

In these two papers I have attempted to deal with a very ob-scure subject, full of subtle distinctions; and I can say with truth that I have found the task by no means an easy one. It might have been done much better — I know that; but at least I have done my best, unsatisfactory though it be, and I cannot help thinking that a careful and long-suffering reader will be able to follow me. There *is* something of very real value to the student of occultism in this record of my research — so I firmly believe; but I readily admit that my pineal symbolism may be very misleading if mistaken for literal fact, and that I am probably quite ignorant of the real nature of my discovery. I use the word "discovery" because it was one for *me*. Well, I have shirked the task of writing about this, and sundry other occult matters, for a good many years — it was too much trouble. But a short while ago, when it seemed most surely that my "number was up," I regretted my procrastination. I got a sense of *waste*. After all, if I tell the little I have done and seen, and my equally obscure brethren do likewise, it all adds to the mass of available data; and then one day Mr. Mastermind can come along and work on it and tell us just what we have been doing, what it really means. Hence these articles.

PART THREE:
DREAM-TRAVELLING

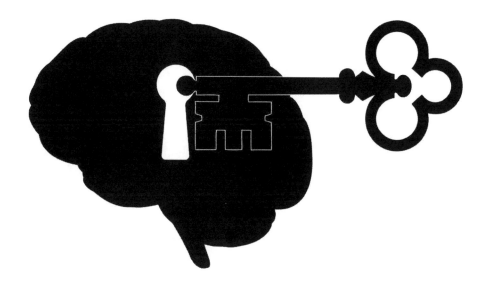

Some Additional Notes

In "The Pineal Doorway" and "Beyond the Pineal Door" I dealt fairly comprehensively with my experiments, extending over many years, in dream-travelling. My object in this present article is to consider an entirely new selection of examples from my records, expanding certain details with which I was forced to deal very briefly in the general scheme of my previous contributions. At the same time, I hope, without being guilty of tedious repetition, I shall bring out the salient points of the former articles, to meet the requirements of new readers. To begin with, I would emphasize two facts:

(a) There is an alternative to the dream-travelling theory: namely, that the methods I have adopted merely induce a third state of consciousness, which differs from both waking life and ordinary dream, and is far more vivid than either.

(b) In the opinion of some occultists, such experiments are dangerous and may lead to obsession, madness, heart-failure, and premature burial.

The final result of my experiments may be stated as follows: I was able to induce a condition of trance, leave my body, travel, return to it, break the trance, and resume normal life — with, seemingly, no gap in consciousness throughout the whole experiment. I will now give a synopsis of the various stages of the research.

(1) I found that in some dreams the perception of an incongruity in my surroundings would give me the knowledge that I was dreaming. I called these "Dreams of Knowledge" to distinguish them from the ordinary kind.

(2) I found that the knowledge of dreaming immediately altered the quality of the dream. I felt in an almost ecstatic state of spiritual well-being and mental clarity. The scenery, however prosaic, instantly became radiant with a divine glamour beyond words. In short, these dreams of knowledge seemed more real and vivid than the happiest moments of waking life.

(3) I found also that this knowledge of dreaming tended to bring the dream to a speedy end. The physical body seemed to be roused into activity and to exercise a magnetic attraction; so that, after a few moments of glorious adventure in this new freedom, my body hauled me back abruptly, like an angry parent capturing a truant schoolboy.

(4) I found that, by exercising my will, I could resist the body and considerably prolong the dream; but that the effort produced a slowly-increasing pain in what I imagined to be the region of the pineal gland.

(5) I made the experiment of fighting this pain. It ceased quite suddenly, and something seemed to click in my head; but I then appeared to be in the position of a permanently disembodied spirit. My body ceased to exercise any attraction; the dream-world seemed more real than this, but no one took any notice of my presence. I argued that, as will-power had got me out, will-power would get me back again. After several attempts I returned to my body, only to find that, though I could hear sounds about the house, I could not move even a little finger. Again by concentration, slowly and painfully, I broke this trance; but the after-effects were bad.

(6) I learnt also from the above experiment that, when near to my body, I experienced a most curious effect of dual consciousness. I could feel myself lying on the bed, hear physical sounds, and dimly see the objects in the room; and simultaneously I could feel myself standing and see the dream surroundings.

(7) The next step was very important. I found that a dream of knowledge very often led to a False Awakening. I would think that I was awake in my room, but feel strange pains and hear terrifying voices. I would also see apparitions, beautiful or hideous, human or non-human, until fright broke the trance, and I was really awake. I called this state the "Trance Condition."

(8) I learnt through many experiments that this horrible trance condition was the all-important factor — the fear had to be conquered, the phantoms faced.

(9) I found that, when in this trance condition, it was possible to leave the body by a sudden will effort. Generally, though not invariably, I was whirled away at tremendous speed and had but little control over my movements. The experience was always of

very brief duration, and the results were decidedly inferior to those obtained by prolonging a dream of knowledge. Also this new method always entailed a momentary break in consciousness. For a long time I was puzzled by the seeming inferiority of the results obtained *via* the trance condition; for I felt intuitively that the trance was the all-important thing, and that the preliminary dream of knowledge could be dispensed with altogether.

(10) At last I found the right method of leaving the body when in the trance condition. I had to will that my incorporeal self should pass *through the doorway of the pineal gland*. When this was done, the little "click" sounded in my brain. There was no being whirled away, no break in consciousness. Calmly and leisurely I could "get up" out of my body and go forth on my adventures. I could travel at what speed I pleased, walk, float, or levitate; pass through walls, or make objects support me (so that I could sit on a chair). There was no restricting "pineal" pain as in the Dream of Knowledge method, and there was no difficulty in re-entering my body when I wished. This was *the* method at last!

(11) As long as my body remained in the trance I was free, but I found it was necessary for me to preserve the calm, dispassionate attitude of an investigator. If I gave way to human emotions of any strength, the trance was instantly broken by what seemed to be a repercussion effect, and I was drawn back in a flash. When my body showed signs of recovering, I found that it was possible for me to enter it very gently, strengthen the trance by concentration, and then go out again — all without any break in consciousness.

(12) The last step was the discovery that by concentration it was possible, though extremely difficult, to produce the trance condition straight away, so I could pass from waking life out of the body and return with seemingly no break in the continuity of perceptions.

I now propose to select from my notebook examples to illustrate these stages. The first is of a Dream of Knowledge.

Ex. 1. In my dream, B (my wife) and I awoke, got up, and dressed. On pulling up the blind, we were amazed to discover that, in place of the row of houses opposite, there were now bare fields. I said to B: "Well, this means that I am dreaming, though everything seems so real and I feel perfectly awake. Those houses could not vanish in the night!" But B was unconvinced. I said: "Well, I am prepared to stand by my reasoning powers. I will jump out of the window, and I shall not be hurt." Despite her objections, I opened the window and climbed out on to the sill. I then jumped, and floated gently down into the street. When my feet touched the pavement, I awoke. B had no memory of dreaming.

Dual consciousness, the false awakening, illusions of the trance condition, and development of astral sight are illustrated in Examples 2 and 3.

Ex. 2. Dozing one afternoon upon the sofa, I experienced the false awakening, imagining that B and two old friends were sitting in the room and talking. I felt too tired to take any part in this conversation and "went to sleep" again. When I next became aware of my surroundings, I realized that I was in the trance condition and could leave my body. I sat up (out of my body, as it were) and then leisurely got off the sofa. Dual consciousness was very pronounced. Simultaneously I could feel myself lying on the sofa and standing by it, my legs pressing against the edge; but though I could see the room quite clearly, I could not see the body I had just left. I walked slowly round the room to the door, the sense of dual consciousness diminishing as I moved away from the sofa; but before I could leave the room, my body pulled me back, and I was awake.

For the inferior method, separation was unusually gentle (see par. 9 above); indeed I suspect that I passed through the pineal door during the break in consciousness; but the duration was very brief.

Ex. 3. After sunset I lay down on the sofa to experiment. My eyes were closed, but presently I could see the room quite plainly — with B sitting, sewing, by the fire — which told me that I was in the trance condition. I then left my body and passed out of the house and into the lamp-lit street. I walked a short distance and entered a grocer's shop; this was full of customers, but no one took any notice of me. I wished to see whether I should be visible to the grocer; but my body called me back, and I thought that I woke. My room seemed just as real as in waking life, but at this moment a brightly-plumaged parrot flew over my head. I then knew this was a false awakening, and that I was still in the trance — which was broken by some noise before I could experiment further.

Ex. 4. Afternoon. Deck-chair. Induced trance condition after break in consciousness. Astral sight. I willed to ascend. Suddenly I was wafted out of my body, turned so that I faced it, and borne upwards in a position almost horizontal. In this rapid passage upwards I saw my face as though viewed from only an inch away, strange and monstrous, and through the eyelids the eyeballs were visible, rolled up and showing only the whites. This apparition was so gruesome that I was badly scared. Nevertheless, I continued to will to ascend and shot up into blackness. Then, when I was considering the next step, the trance ended.

This is one of the very rare cases where I have been able to see my body. As a rule, I believe a sort of downwards clairvoyance is necessary to see physical objects, as distinct from their astral counterparts. It may have been due to the unusual way in which separation was effected.

The remaining examples are of attempts to obtain separation by the superior method of passing through the pineal door.

Ex. 5 illustrates the breaking of the trance by a repercussion effect.

Ex. 5. Afternoon. Sofa. Induced trance condition after break in consciousness. Could see the room very clearly. Strong "outrush or uprush" sensations as in Ex. 6. Separation excellently effected. Dual consciousness until I left the room. I walked downstairs. Then I was caught up and carried away to a great oriental (?) palace, where a beautiful girl was dancing before an assembly of richly-dressed reclining men and women. No one could see me. I stood before the dancer and looked right into her sky-blue eyes, but she took no notice. Foolishly succumbing to my curiosity, I touched her bare, warm arm. She started so violently that the shock induced in me broke the trance, and I was instantly rushed back to my body.

Ex. 6 illustrates the complete method of inducing the trance and leaving the body without break in consciousness.

Ex. 6. On this occasion I experimented with the definite object of visiting a new friend, whose house I had not seen, though I knew the address. On retiring for the night, I kept my body as still as possible, taking deep rhythmic breaths. I did not concentrate on my friend, but on the preliminary stages of the experiment, as I wished to avoid any break in consciousness. In this I was quite successful. After the breathing had continued for some time, I noted a sensation in my physical eyes, as though they were rolled upwards and squinting slightly. At the same time all my consciousness seemed to be focused upon a point situated in the middle of the front part of my brain. Soon I began to feel a numbness stealing over my body, extending from the feet upwards and gradually stiffening into a state resembling catalepsy, even my jaws being bound together, as though with iron bands. I was still in darkness, my eyes being tightly closed; but now came the sensation of possessing another pair, and these astral eyes I opened. I was lying on my right side and facing B. As I opened these other eyes, I seemed to turn right round within my physical body, so that I faced the other direction. Great forces seemed to be straining the atmosphere, and bluish-green flashes of light came from all parts of the room.

I then caught sight of a hideous monster — a vague, white, filmy, formless thing, spreading out in queer patches, with bulbous protuberances and snake-like tentacles. It had two enormous round eyes, like globes filled with pale-blue fire, each about six or seven inches in diameter. I felt my heart leap, and my breathing changed to jerky gaspings. I turned over again within my body, and, telling myself that nothing could harm me, concentrated on strengthening the trance. When I had recovered from the shock, I turned once more. The monster had gone, but the flashings continued for a little while. These, too, subsided, and the room seemed as usual, except that it was dimly and evenly illuminated by no visible source of light.

I willed to leave my body. I had the sensation of my incorporeal self rushing towards and being condensed in the pineal region; and at the same time the astral light increased in intensity till it became a vivid golden blaze. I then passed through the pineal door and "got up." I could see B's form, but not my body — so far I have never been able to see this after obtaining separation by the pineal-door method. Dual consciousness ceased after I had left the house; this time I had passed through the doors, without opening their astral counterparts.

I then concentrated on the idea of travelling to my friend's house. Almost immediately I was caught up and borne along with ever-increasing velocity, passing through houses and trees, and apparently taking the shortest line to the goal. I then found myself beating against the fronts of houses resembling those in L. Avenue. I was like a piece of paper blown by a gale hither and thither. The directing impulse seemed to have given out, and I could not find the right house. At this point my body called me back. The trance was not broken and I strengthened it, intending to try again. Then I heard B say with peculiar distinctness: "No!

You must not do it again now, or I shall be frightened." I thought her voice was probably only an illusion and so hesitated. Then she spoke again: "Wake up!" I still thought the voice unreal in the physical sense; but not wishing to risk distressing her, I obeyed. I broke the trance and questioned her. She had not spoken. On visiting my friend next day, I recognized the houses on either side of hers as being those I had tried to enter.

Conclusion

I will conclude this article by anticipating certain questions which the critical reader may well ask: Do these experiments prove anything? Could they be repeated by other students? Is there any real good in attempting such admittedly dangerous practices? Is the game worth the candle?

I know from the experiences of my wife and friends, and people who have written with reference to my former contributions, that it is possible for others to obtain the knowledge that they are dreaming and to prolong the dream. I also know that many students can obtain separation by what I have called the inferior method; but I have never met with a description of my pineal-door method. And here I would again emphasize that its superiority lies in the fact that one is not whirled away at the moment of separation and so does not experience a break in consciousness. However, it is true that after I had moved away from my body and left the house, I was always more or less at the mercy of astral currents; but such sudden transitions did not interfere with the apparent continuity of my perceptions. The pineal method also possessed this advantage: once the door was passed, it was possible to leave the body and return to it several times without breaking the trance.

And now what do such experiments prove? Well, I think it can be said most positively that in certain dreams (normally of very rare occurrence) the reasoning faculty remains awake, and that such abnormal dreams are accompanied by (or lead to) an abnormal condition of the physical body. The result is a third state of consciousness, as I have said. To prove that the soul actually leaves the body is practically impossible; for the experiences may be purely subjective; and even where the scenes are afterwards verified and the traveller clairvoyantly observed out of his body, the theories of telaesthesia and telepathy can still be advanced. I do not see how the immortality of the soul can be demonstrated conclusively for the satisfaction of all; but, personally, I believe that I have left my body, that — except for the severing of the cord — I have "died" many times.

These experiments have been, perhaps, the strongest influence in my life in fighting a pessimistic, materialistic side to my mentality — that has been their value for me. I know this drab prosaic life I lead at present is only the prelude to a world of glorious adventure, of wisdom, beauty, and divine love. I have proved to my own satisfaction the existence of my soul.

Further Reading

Exploring Your Inner Reality: A Guidebook to Astral Projection and the Out-of-Body Experience by Jonas Ridgeway

The Projection of the Astral Body by Sylvan Muldoon

Journeys Out of the Body by Robert A. Monroe

Far Journeys by Robert A Monroe

Ultimate Journey by Robert A. Monroe

Seth, Dreams, and Projections of Consciousness by Jane Roberts

The Seth Material by Jane Roberts

Seth Speaks by Jane Roberts

The Nature of Personal Reality: A Seth Book by Jane Roberts

Leaving The Body - A Complete Guide To Astral Projection by D. Scott Rogo

Out-of-Body Adventures: 30 Days to the Most Exciting Experience of Your Life by Rick Stack

Out-of-Body Experiences: How to Have Them and What to Expect by Robert Peterson

Adventures Beyond the Body: How to Experience Out-of-Body Travel by William Buhlman

About the Author

Oliver Fox (the pseudonym of Hugh George Callaway) is one of the pioneers of astral projection and the out-of-body experience. He was born November 30th, 1885, and died April 28th, 1949. He is the author of *Astral Projection: A Record of Out-of-the-Body Experiences*.

THE END

Made in the USA
Middletown, DE
15 September 2024

60984187R00050